Cyber Security for Procurement: A Guide to Protecting Business

I0003833

Contents

Cyber Security for Procurement: A Guide to Protect your Business

BACKGROUND

The importance of cybersecurity has increased in recent years due to factors such as apparent breaches in the business and political realms. Individual practices regarding cybersecurity, such as the creation of strong passwords, multi-step authentication, and the need for healthy skepticism and awareness regarding phishing attempts, have gained public recognition to the point of becoming common knowledge, but risks continue to evolve.

Fortunately, there is ready access to resources and guidance on risk avoidance for individuals, personally and professionally. The advice in this book is offered to counter the cyber risk faced by procurement professionals, who function as gatekeepers for cybersecurity and must exert due diligence to safeguard procurement operations and the supply chain.

In a world where technology has become an integral part of our daily lives, it's imperative to protect our organizations from the ever-growing threat of cyber risks. In this book, we delve into the critical work of Procurement and how to safeguard against cyber threats and address the vital business function of cybersecurity as early as possible.

Through real-life experiences and expert insights, this book provides a comprehensive understanding of Procurement and how to identify, prevent, and respond to cyber risks.

Cyber Security for Procurement: A Guide to Protect your Business

This book covers all aspects of procurement cybersecurity, from vendor risk management to data protection, and offers practical solutions for securing your organization.

Whether you are a seasoned procurement professional or new to the field, this book is a must-read for anyone looking to stay ahead of the ever-evolving cyber threat landscape.

Recommended Standard:

The entity's policy should support the development, maintenance, and updating of its cyber security plan, which should be included in its Technology Plan and emergency Continuity of Operations Plan (COOP). The plans may consist of sections specific to each department but should be kept together in a single comprehensive document, allowing for ready access and regular updates. The single repository ensures that information for the entity and its departments is consistent. The focus of this practice is Procurement's role and responsibility for cyber security with the knowledge that throughout the procurement cycle, Procurement must identify, assess, and address cyber security risks.

Definition:

[*The Computer Security Resource Center (CSRC) for the National Institute of Standards and Technology (NIST) defines cybersecurity as:*

Cybersecurity: Prevention of damage to and protection and restoration of computers, electronic communications systems, electronic communications services, wire communications, and the information contained therein to ensure its availability, integrity, confidentiality, authentication, and nonrepudiation.

Source: https://csrc.nist.gov/glossary/term/cybersecurity

Cyber Security for Procurement: A Guide to Protect your Business

Elements of a Procurement Cybersecurity Program

Element 1: The Procurement professional should work with Cybersecurity Department and other stakeholders to identify cyber risks pertaining to procurement operations and functions and understand any additional regulatory or legal requirements the proposed solution must meet based on the type of information processed.

The global best practice "The Place of Public Procurement within the Entity" describes Procurement as a liaison to all other departments. Procurement should identify its operations and functions and collaborate with their agency I.T. Security Department and other stakeholders to determine the types and levels of cyber risk pertaining to Procurement.

Procurement professionals may encounter cyber risk in areas such as:

- Software or services that are not fully capable of meeting all agency or regulatory security requirements
- Security gaps in the vendor's internal security practices
- Counterfeit software embedded with malware
- Outsourced procurement functions
- Untested or unreliable software packages
- Vulnerabilities within new or legacy systems
- Incompatibility among systems

Cyber Security for Procurement: A Guide to Protect your Business

- Use of contractors, sub-contractors, and third and other parties, including issues of:
    - Location, e.g., parties outside the U.S.
    - Unauthorized access to the system
    - Federally banned parties, e.g., Huawei

Cyber risk continues to evolve due to technology's continual evolution, innovation, and corresponding vulnerabilities and cyber attacks. Examples of vulnerabilities include:

- Standardized technologies.
- Insecure connections and links to unsecured networks.
- Publicly available system manuals.
- Insufficient staff training on best practices for the use of technology.
- Inconsistent security practices among stakeholders, i.e., insufficient and inconsistent policies, procedures, and processes.

Other factors that affect risk include:

- Complexity and proximity of an event
- Number and type of stakeholders (internal, external, third party)
- The ability to identify and respond to security breaches
- Rate of innovation
- Age of hardware and software and implementation of updates, patches
- Rigor and frequency of training
- Process of vetting contractors

Cyber Security for Procurement: A Guide to Protect your Business

- Level of confidentiality/security/privacy

- Processes used, e.g., procurement cards, credit cards, third-party procurement services

- Systems used, e.g., level of connection and integration to other systems

- Contract terms and conditions

The number of risk factors, the inherent risk, and the complexity of each element, individually or in combination, affect the risk's resultant severity/harm level. See the Zones of Cyber Risk graphic.

Cyber Security for Procurement: A Guide to Protect your Business

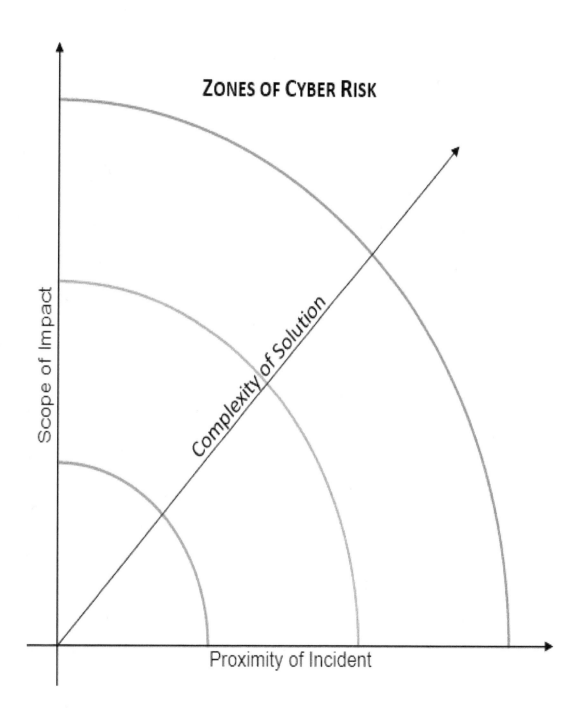

ZONES OF CYBER RISK

Scope of Impact

Complexity of Solution

Proximity of Incident

Cyber Security for Procurement: A Guide to Protect your Business

Element 2: The procurement professional must recognize the unique risks of each contract and establish processes and procedures to address cyber security in the supply chain.

From the beginning of the procurement cycle, i.e., identifying a need, the procurement professional must collaborate with the customer to identify potential risks. The procurement professional should also have full knowledge of the types of data that will be processed and should coordinate with agency security and privacy teams to ensure that these requirements are included in any proposal submitted to the proposed vendor. The solicitation and resulting contract can help to mitigate or contribute to risk. Attention should be given to potential cyber security risks by contractors and subcontractors. Contractors and subcontractors can introduce vulnerabilities, for example, by sharing login information and using weak passwords. Examples of risk presented by contractors and subcontractors include the location of stored data, responding to phishing attempts, or using outdated software and not keeping up with the installation of new versions and patches—lack of security and virus protection software deployed and maintained on user machines. Policies and training must address contractor and third-party vulnerabilities. Risk can be mitigated through a written scope of work and specifications, contract terms and conditions, minimum qualifications, supplier vetting and training, and other practices. The vendor's internal security policies and procedures and the controls within the proposed

Cyber Security for Procurement: A Guide to Protect your Business

solution must be clearly defined to ensure that the solution is fully capable of meeting the stated security requirements.

The vulnerabilities and risks identified in collaboration with I.T. and other stakeholders should serve as a framework for Procurement to develop policies and training regarding prevention, response, and recovery from cyber security incidents.

Cyber Security for Procurement: A Guide to Protect your Business

Element 3: Procurement professionals must ensure that the vendor has established appropriate cyber security policies that provide the authority for daily due diligence and mandatory training of persons assigned to develop applications, as well as manage applications and infrastructure used to store and process agency data.

Policies should add rigor to protect records and credentials, strengthen applications and operating system software to rebuff unauthorized access, and add security measures, e.g., using passwords, encryption, and training in good cybersecurity practices. Policies should also establish authority for roles and responsibilities for incorporating cyber security into procurement processes.

The procurement professional must work with I.T. to determine the type of information and systems that must be secured. Cyber security plans should relate to and be supported by policies and training. Policies and training may result from federal or state statutes and requirements for privacy and security, such as the Health Insurance Portability and Accountability Act (HIPPA), the Family Educational Rights and Privacy Act (FERPA), and the Internal Revenue Service Publication 1075, Safeguards for Protecting Federal Tax Information, as well as existing agency-specific requirements. Policies and training should also consider vulnerable periods of developing, updating or replacing any system or software. I.T. provides expertise in technology, and Procurement delivers expertise in the procurement process and supply chain. Procurement and I.T. should collaborate to

Cyber Security for Procurement: A Guide to Protect your Business

monitor systems regularly, perform system checks, security and risk assessments, penetration testing and report, updates, and develop the Procurement section of the entity's technology plan. Policies and training should address the following:

- Mandatory, regular training in safe, intelligent technology practices, e.g., strong passwords.

- Required agreements for data sharing and system interconnections.

- Establishment of a regularly updated cyber security plan.

- Protection of confidential and personal identifying information (PII).

- Processes and procedures to ensure cyber security in the supply chain.

- Monitoring and assessing key suppliers to ensure they meet cyber security performance and training standards, e.g., (NOTE: the U.S. has not yet adopted GDPR) National Institute of Standards and Technology (NIST), ISO 27001, ISAE 3000.

As noted in Information Technology (I.T.) Procurement Series — No. 2, *procurement professionals function as liaisons to other departments and must understand the concepts, unique attributes, and language of I.T. Terms with which public procurement professionals should be familiar include:*
- *Cyber risk*
- *Cyber liability*
- *Cyber liability insurance, cyber risk insurance, cyber breach insurance*
- *Data breach vs. Security Incident*
- *Technology Professional Liability*
- *Control systems*
Definitions for these and other related terms may be found in NIST: National Institute of Standards and Technology: https://www.nist.gov/

Cyber Security for Procurement: A Guide to Protect your Business

Protect confidential and personal identifying information (PII).

PII breaches can originate internally, for example, through procurement cards, or externally, through government acceptance of credit cards from customers. To protect confidential and PII information, Procurement should:

- Separate the entity's procurement card system environment from its email environment.

- Implement stricter controls, e.g., limited access by suppliers, specific activation and deactivation of access to the system

- Conduct Payment Card Industry (PCI) Audits

- Include contract language in Requests for Information (RFI) and Requests for Proposals (RFP)

> ***Example: PCI Compliance*** *– During the term of this Agreement, (Company Name) shall ensure compliance with the latest version of the Payment Card Industry - Data Security Standard (PCI DSS), including any associated amendments or restatements. (Company Name) accepts responsibility for the security of customer credit card data in its possession, even if all or a portion of the services are subcontracted to third parties. Upon request by the Subscriber, (Company Name) shall be required to provide evidence of PCI DSS compliance.*

When developing solicitation documents, the scope of work, specifications, evaluation criteria, terms and conditions, and onboarding and monitoring of contractors should incorporate cyber security considerations. To mitigate risk in the supply chain, Procurement should:

- Use consistent and plain language for requirements.
  - Each requirement should include no more than one criterion

Cyber Security for Procurement: A Guide to Protect your Business

- o Conjunctions and conditional statements should be avoided
- Require contractors to undergo an onboarding process with specific cyber security training and accountability for compliance.
- Require contractors to review and sign a non-disclosure security agreement annually.
- Conduct risk assessments for each prospective contractor, sub-contractor, and third party by:
  - o Checking for debarment or suspension
  - o Asking about their approach to data security and which protective systems they use
  - o Requiring an insurance certificate that covers the following:
    - Network security liability
    - Privacy liability
    - Website/digital assets liability
    - Breach management
    - Privacy notification
    - Business interruption
    - Third-party activities
  - o Ensuring that the supplier has conducted a penetration test and has website certificate insurance
  - o Requiring specific and relevant certification such as ISO, ISEA, or SOC before being awarded the contract.

Cyber Security for Procurement: A Guide to Protect your Business

- o For vendor cloud solutions, determine whether the data stored is in the Public or GOV Cloud. If the data is stored in the GOV Cloud, is the vendor FedRamp certified?

- Develop contract clauses that are written and appropriate to each Procurement.

- View Terms and Conditions as modifiable, including boilerplate terms and conditions.

- Ensure that contract clauses address the location of contractors, servers, data, data ownership, and insurance.

Procurement professionals should also be alert to the potential cybersecurity risks inherent in other purchased products and services. Technology in vehicles, security cameras, audio-visual devices, and building maintenance services could introduce cybersecurity vulnerabilities in the organization.

Increasingly, entities are hiring an outside firm, consultant, or university to assess the entity's systems and processes regarding cyber security and vulnerabilities. Similarly, insurance companies increasingly require suppliers to verify that their systems, processes, and subcontractors qualify to maintain certification.

Cyber Security for Procurement: A Guide to Protect your Business

Element 4: The unique requirements of Procurement should be addressed in the entity's regularly updated cyber security plan for response to and recovery from an incident or event.

The development of a cohesive cybersecurity plan requires coordination between all departments. Procurement should collaborate with the I.T. department to ensure that Procurement's roles, responsibilities, procedures, and processes are included and align with the entity's cyber security plan. To address risk in Procurement operations, technology, the procurement cycle, and the supply chain, i.e., contractors, sub-contractors, and third parties, the cyber security plan should include best practices and processes for cyber risk avoidance, identification, prevention, mitigation, assessment, response, and resilience. The cyber security plan should incorporate the types and levels of risk defined with I.T. as well as established policies and procedures.

In general, a cyber security plan should include the following:

- Common language: Adopt terminology from NIST to facilitate effective communication and coordination.

- Points of contact: Base authority for a cyber breach or incident on expertise and establish multiple contact points for communication redundancy, i.e., backup. Points of connection may differ from the daily hierarchy.
  - Establish emergency responders for your organization, i.e., Incident Response Team Management

Cyber Security for Procurement: A Guide to Protect your Business

- Team structures, individual roles and responsibilities, escalation processes, and protocols, including decision authority, for different types and levels of incidents or events.
  - Backup/redundancy strategies and actions for each person and function
- Links between actions and performance measures, e.g., recognizing the type of incident or event and measuring response time.
- Checklists.
- Processes for continuous improvement, e.g., lessons learned, tracking industry, legislation, benchmarking, and implementation.

Consequences of cyber events generally affect the following areas:
- Financial
- Legal
- Security/Privacy
- Reputation/Brand

Cyber Security for Procurement: A Guide to Protect your Business

Element 5: Standards are essential in developing specifications that produce the desired, relevant response without being onerous to the proposers and evaluators.

In current practice, suppliers are sometimes required to respond to hundreds of questions for the entity to determine that the supplier meets a standard of cyber security reliability. Independently audited supplier certifications assure entities that suppliers have met such criteria.

Requirements/standards specific to organizations

Procurement can provide a set of questions/requirements to ask / demand in solicitations to gauge the security of software solutions their agency intends to contract. Norwich University has an excellent example of such an approach, it's Higher Education Community Vendor Assessment Tool (HECVAT). The advantage of such an approach is that it is specific to organizations (in this case, Universities). The disadvantage is that it requires expertise to set (and maintain) those standards. For suppliers, it is onerous to respond, and their answers may be complex for the agency to verify.

Industry standards that can be independently audited (ISO, ISEA, SOC)

Different groups of independent experts under different governance have been gathering standards for hundreds of segments, including information security. The advantages of such standards are that they are set and maintained by global experts, while software solutions and vendors can independently be verified against those standards.

ISO 27001

ISO 27001 is a risk-based standard for establishing, implementing, and improving an organization's security framework or "ISMS." This standard framework is maintained by information security professionals at the ISO and IEC. The implemented ISO 27001 framework is certified by independent certification bodies. ISO 27001 is a complete system for assuring information security; All organizations that implemented ISO 27001 have a solid strategy for managing information security. An ISO 27001 certification is often required when contracting a SaaS solution.

ISAE 3000 / SOC 2

ISAE (3000) / SOC 2 is similar to ISO 27001 but also examines how risks have been managed. It avoids a situation in which controls are formally implemented but ineffective. An ISAE 3000 / SOC2 audit is an in-depth audit focusing on the effectiveness of the risk framework in managing risks. If risks are not effectively managed, it is exposed in the ISAE report. This level of transparency is required in the global economy and the continually evolving threat landscape. An ISAE 3000 / SOC 2 certification is often needed when contracting a SaaS solution.

Cyber Security for Procurement: A Guide to Protect your Business

U.S. Federal government standards (FISMA, FedRAMP)

When becoming FISMA compliant, organizations are awarded authorization to operate (ATO) from the specific federal agency, considered a one-to-one process. This means that each agency can have different requirements because of the unique needs that an agency may have. Thus multiple ATOs from multiple agencies must be maintained to keep specific federal contracts.

When becoming FedRAMP compliant, organizations are awarded an ATO that can be leveraged by any federal agency, which supports a "do once, use many" framework. FedRAMP, because of this framework, is more rigorous as it is intended to be used by any agency. In addition, FedRAMP is specifically designed for the assessment of SaaS providers.

- o Does the contractor, sub-contractor, third-party meet performance and training standards, e.g., (NOTE: the U.S. has not yet adopted GDPR) NIST? (These must be stated in the solicitation.)
- Implement an onboarding process for new suppliers, e.g., pull from JMARK

A supplier's cybersecurity practices should be treated similarly to its quality or delivery performance. Buyers should be empowered to end the relationship if the vendor cannot meet sufficient performance levels.

Cyber Security for Procurement: A Guide to Protect your Business

Conclusion

An organization's procurement office and program are paramount in securing your organization. Cybersecurity advocates speak on including security as early as possible in designing and procuring solutions. The elements included in this book provide the foundation for building a cyber-resilient and reduced-risk organization.

Applying these practices further benefits the organization through established standards that contribute to reducing time in onboarding and procuring solutions and vendors. We now have the answers to the, what are our standards? What should we ask of the vendors?

If you found this book helpful, please leave a review. If you require additional assistance, please reach out to Leber Consulting. Review the RFP language examples, and the elements cybersecurity seeks in vendor management in Appendix A and B.

drleber@leberconsultingllc.com

www.leberconsultingllc.com

Cyber Security for Procurement: A Guide to Protect your Business

References:

"Christchurch Call | to Eliminate Terrorist and Violent Extremist Content Online." Accessed January 24, 2023. https://www.christchurchcall.com/.

NASPO.org. "Cyber Liability Insurance 101." Accessed January 24, 2023. https://www.naspo.org/Publications/ArtMID/8806/ArticleID/3403.

"Cybersecurity & Supply Chain Risk Management | FAI.GOV." Accessed January 24, 2023. https://www.fai.gov/topics/cybersecurity-supply-chain-risk-management.

"Cybersecurity – What Does It Mean For Procurement In 2019? - Blog | Procurious." Accessed January 24, 2020. https://www.procurious.com/procurement-news/cybersecurity-what-does-it-mean-for-procurement-in-2019.

Editor, CSRC Content. "Home | CSRC." Accessed January 24, 2023. https://csrc.nist.gov/.

"Enterprise Security Policies and Standards." Accessed January 24, 2023. https://www.its.ms.gov/Services/Pages/ENTERPRISE-SECURITY-POLICY.aspx.

Financial Services Sector Coordinating Council. "Purchaser's Guide to Cyber Insurance Products," 2016. https://fsscc.org/files/galleries/FSSCC_Cyber_Insurance_Purchasers_Guide_FINAL-TLP_White.pdf.

Foxman, Stephen. "Sample Contract Clauses." Eckert Seamans, n.d. https://www.eckertseamans.com/app/uploads/Steve-Foxman_Eckert-Seamans_DATA-PROTECTION-CLAUSES-101016-M1566466xA35AF.pdf.

JMark Business Solutions, Inc. "Your Cybersecurity Checklist," n.d. https://www.jmark.com/wp-content/uploads/2018/10/Cybersecurity-Checklist.pdf.

"Mississippi Enterprise Security Program Provides Framework for Agency Partnerships." Accessed January 24, 2023. https://www.govtech.com/security/Mississippi-Enterprise-Security-Program-Provides-Framework-for-Agency-Partnerships.html.

"National Cybersecurity Awareness Month Resources | CISA." Accessed January 24, 2023. https://www.cisa.gov/publication/national-cyber-security-awareness-month-resources.

Cyber Security for Procurement: A Guide to Protect your Business

NIGP: The InstituteInstittue for Public Procurement. "Information Technology Series No. 1," n.d. https://www.nigp.org/docs/default-source/new-site/global-best-practices/it-procurement-practice---series-1.pdf?sfvrsn=7132917a_0.

———. "Information Technology Series No. 2 - I.T. Procurement," n.d. https://www.nigp.org/docs/default-source/new-site/global-best-practices/it-procurement-software.pdf?sfvrsn=8a56917a_0.

———. "Information Technology Series No. 3 Hardware," n.d. https://www.nigp.org/docs/default-source/new-site/global-best-practices/it-procurement-series-3-hardware-final-2.pdf?sfvrsn=9a56917a_0.

———. "Information Technology Series No. 4 Services," n.d. https://www.nigp.org/docs/default-source/new-site/global-best-practices/it-procurement-series-no-4---services-non-professional-support-and-maintenance-cloud.pdf?sfvrsn=f3911b76_0.

"Pennsylvania Specialists Share Cybersecurity Tips." Accessed January 24, 2023. https://www.govtech.com/security/Pennsylvania-Specialists-Share-Cybersecurity-Tips.html.

Rogers, Zac, and Thomas Y. Choi. "Purchasing Managers Have a Lead Role to Play in Cyber Defense." *Harvard Business Review*, July 10, 2018. https://hbr.org/2018/07/purchasing-managers-have-a-lead-role-to-play-in-cyber-defense.
"Texas Towns Slammed in 'Coordinated' Ransomware Attack." Accessed January 24, 2020. https://www.govtech.com/security/Texas-Towns-Slammed-in-Coordinated-Ransomware-Attack.html.

Appendix A: Example of RFP language for cybersecurity

Suggested additional requirements to supplement the VENDOR

SOW

Compliance with <your organization> I.T. Enterprise Policy and Standards

The VENDOR solution shall adhere to Federal and <your organization> standards as

outlined below:

A. The <your organization> Office of Technology (<YOUR ORGANIZATION>) I.T. Enterprise

Policy and Standards provide guidelines, policies, directional statements, and sets of

standards so that technology choices can be made based on business objectives and

service delivery. These documents are located here:

- <YOUR ORGANIZATION> Standards:

- <YOUR ORGANIZATION> Policies:

B. <YOUR ORGANIZATION> Policy and Standards reflect a set of principles for

information, technology, applications, and organization which shall be followed for any

solution hosted and maintained by VENDOR. <YOUR ORGANIZATION> also has standards

Cyber Security for Procurement: A Guide to Protect your Business

to which any solution hosted and maintained by VENDOR shall adhere. These documents are located here:

- <YOUR ORGANIZATION> Standards:

- <YOUR ORGANIZATION> Policies:

C. If the VENDOR solution components hosted and maintained by VENDOR deviate from the Policies and Standards referenced above, VENDOR shall outline the reasons and benefits to the <your organization> for that deviation. Any exceptions to these Policies and Standards must follow the <YOUR ORGANIZATION>.

Compliance with Federal Regulations and Standards

VENDOR shall ensure that its work under this contract, including all deliverables, will meet the requirements of all applicable federal and state laws, regulations, policies, and guidance, including any amendments or updates during the contract's life. Adherence to these laws, policies, regulations, and guidance shall be a requirement of the VENDOR solution.

The relevant laws, regulations, policies, and guidance include, but are not limited to:

- Title XIX of the Social Security Act, the Medicaid statute

- The Office of the National Health Coordinator for Health Information Technology

Cyber Security for Procurement: A Guide to Protect your Business

- Health Insurance Portability and Accountability Act (HIPAA) and any related regulations and guidance

- Medicaid Information Technology Architecture (MITA) CMS Minimum Acceptable Risk Standards for Exchanges (MARS-E) v2.0

- List State Statutes

- NIST Special Publication SP800-53 R4 Security and Privacy Controls for Federal Information Systems and Organizations

Privacy, Confidentiality, and Ownership of Information

<YOUR ORGANIZATION> is the designated owner of all data and shall approve all access to that data. VENDOR shall not have ownership of <your organization> data at any time. VENDOR shall comply with privacy policies established by governmental agencies or state or federal law. Privacy policy statements may be developed and amended periodically by <your organization>.

Security Testing:

Security Testing is required by VENDOR on functional, technical, and infrastructure components to ensure the system meets all system security requirements. Testing is required whenever significant system changes occur. Security Testing scenarios and strategy shall be approved by the <YOUR ORGANIZATION> Security Team before execution, and all Security Testing results shall be validated by <YOUR ORGANIZATION> and the <YOUR ORGANIZATION> Security Team.

Penetration Testing shall be performed by VENDOR, with subsequent validation performed by the <YOUR ORGANIZATION> Penetration Testing Team.

VENDOR shall support and participate in, as required, Control Assessments, HIPAA Risk Assessments, or other security-related Assessments.

Weaknesses or findings (as identified by audit or other assessment methods) shall be documented in a <YOUR ORGANIZATION> -prescribed Plan of Action and Milestones (POAM) template. VENDOR shall maintain and remediate POAMs and provide monthly status updates to designated <your organization> personnel. Any necessary exception (due to business, technical, or other limitations) that impacts the resolution of a POAM must follow the <YOUR ORGANIZATION>.

POAM remediation timelines (from the date of Weakness, Vulnerability, or Gap Identified):

- High-Risk POAM Items   30 Days

- Moderate Risk POAM Items 6 Months

- Low-Risk POAM Items   1 Year

Cyber Security for Procurement: A Guide to Protect your Business

Appendix B: Checklist against a vendor management program (VMP)

The elements a Cybersecurity Department looks for in a mature Vendor Management

Program (VMP):

The goals of the I.S. Department in the vendor, contract, and RFP process is to:

1. Manage Vendor Relationships

2. Complete Due Diligence

3. Clearly Define cybersecurity expectations & responsibilities

4. Ongoing monitoring

Items to implement a VMP:

- Classification of Vendors by criticality of their business process

- A list of all vendors, what their purpose is, and what they have access to

These two steps provide the groundwork for prioritizing the review, level of assessment,

and requirements we apply to vendors.

The factors cybersecurity looks to assess vendors are:

1. Operational Risk; what impact on the business would/does this vendor present

Cyber Security for Procurement: A Guide to Protect your Business

2. Privacy Risk; What type of data does the vendor have access to, e.g., PII, ePHI

3. Reputation Risk; what impact on our organization's reputation could this vendor have

4. Security Risk; how is data shared, assessed, stored, and destroyed

5. Regulatory Risk; what exposures does this vendor open us up to, and are adequate protections in place

6. Revenue Risk; if service is lost from the vendor, how do we continue business

7. Financial risk; what financial exposures does this vendor expose our organization to, fines, fees, cost to migrate to another vendor if required

8. Service Risk; do they have 24x7 access

Items from a cybersecurity point of view that we would want to see/addressed in contracts are;

- How do we verify vendor has security controls in place

- Obligation to protect our organization, and our data

- Obligations to access data

- Risk assessments

- Background checks

Cyber Security for Procurement: A Guide to Protect your Business

- NDAs

- DR & BCP (disaster recovery & business continuity plans)

- Response plans, expected alert times of breaches, notification escalation procedures, Incident response plan

- Opt out parameters for our organization if the vendor fails to meet expectations

- Certifications, i.e., SOC2, SSAE 16, etc.

- Right to Audit

- How vendor will handle our data

- Compliance expectations, i.e., HIPAA

- SLAs

- Terms of our organization's conducting audits & monitoring

- Enforcement mechanisms

- Shared obligations (HIPAA/BAA)